LOST LINES OF ENGLAND
MATLOCK TO BUXTON

G. P. ESSEX

GRAFFEG

CONTENTS

Foreword	3
Introduction	5
Matlock	15
Darley Dale	18
Rowsley	22
Bakewell	30
Hassop	34
Great Longstone	37
Monsal Dale	43
Millers Dale	44
Blackwell Mill Halt	55
Buxton	59

FOREWORD

The Peak District was already a busy industrial area before the railway between Buxton and Matlock arrived. Extensive mining of coal, lead, copper and other minerals, along with limestone quarrying, had brought tramways and canals to the area since the late 18th century.

There was also some tourism in the area, which was known for its scenery and landscape. The philosopher Thomas Hobbes wrote his famous poem and touring description *The Seven Wonders of the Peak* in 1636.

Buxton was settled by the Romans around 78 CE, when it was known as Aquae Arnemetiae – the spa of the goddess of the grove – due to its geothermal spring, which rises at a constant temperature of 28°C.

It gained importance in the 18th century, when developments by the 5th Duke of Devonshire, using profits from copper mining, made it a popular alternative to Bath as a spa town.

The line that this book covers, from Matlock to Buxton, was originally opened in 1849 as the Manchester, Buxton, Matlock & Midland Junction Railway, starting at Ambergate, the junction with the main line between Derby and Chesterfield, and running as far as Rowsley. As was often the case with early railways, the company ran out of money and could go no further. After taking a joint lease with the LNWR on the section to Rowsley, the Midland Railway carried on construction and completed the line to Buxton in 1863.

Although the line to Buxton was an important connection to a then busy town, it always remained a branch, due to the opposition of the LNWR against the Midland creating a direct line through Buxton to compete with its own. This meant that the Midland's main line went north of the town, heading to Dove Holes and New Mills, reaching Manchester in 1867.

Although the line survived the 1963 Beeching report, which saw the closure of numerous lines and over 2,000 stations, the section between Matlock and Buxton was closed to passenger traffic in 1967. Despite both Matlock and Buxton stations surviving as part of the main rail network, their connection was severed, which surprised many people, as the line had been a main route to Manchester, with Pullman expresses using the route less than a decade earlier.

Since the mid-1970s the Peak Rail heritage line has operated between Rowlsey and Matlock, with much of the remainder being taken over by the Peak District National Park Authority in 1980 and being turned into the very popular Monsal Trail, a walking and cycling route. There is still freight traffic at the Buxton end of the line, where the Great Rocks freight line is used for limestone haulage via Dove Holes tunnel to Chapel Milton.

INTRODUCTION

This lost line winds through deep cuttings, numerous tunnels and several dramatic viaducts for 19 miles through the southern Peak District. It was, when finally completed, seen as a wonder of Victorian engineering, but had several critics, including the critic and social philosopher John Ruskin.

The original plans were drawn up by the Manchester, Buxton, Matlock & Midland Junction Railway. Their proposal, financially backed by the MR, saw their line running from the main Derby to Chesterfield line, with a junction at Ambergate, heading through the Peak District to Cheadle, where it would meet the Manchester & Birmingham Railway. The original route passed through Cromford, Matlock, Winster, Chatsworth, Bakewell and Buxton. An Act of Parliament was granted on 16th July 1846.

However, the original plans of the MBMMJR were thwarted by numerous events, initially the merger of the M&BR with the Grand Junction and London & Birmingham Railways to form the London & North Western Railway. The LNWR had an intense rivalry with the Midland, and, despite having a shareholding in the MBMMJR, didn't want the proposed railway to be completed, as it saw the line would give the Midland access to Manchester, in direct competition with the LNWR.

Despite the MBMMJR submitting plans for an easier and cheaper route, for which it received a new Act of Parliament in 1847, it still ran into financial difficulties. Consequently, the project ended up finishing part way, as a line from Ambergate to Rowsley, a total of 11½ miles, opening on 4th June 1849. By this time the original company had been merged with the MR. In 1852 the line was leased jointly to the MR and the LNWR.

The Midland intended to continue the MBMMJR's original project and finish the construction through to Manchester. In May 1860 they received Royal Assent for the new route from Rowsley to Buxton. The original MBMMJR route was abandoned, due to an objection from the Duke

Matlock to Buxton 5

of Devonshire, as it went through the parkland surrounding his country seat, Chatsworth House. There was also an objection from the Duke of Rutland, who owned nearby Haddon Hall. Whilst the route did not deviate, it was placed in a shallow cut and cover tunnel at the Duke's insistence, as he objected to the view from Haddon Hall being spoilt by the railway. The shallowest tunnel on the route, it averages only 12 feet deep. A cutting would have been sufficient to preserve the view from Haddon Hall, but the Duke did not want to see smoke and steam rising above his stately gardens, so a tunnel, complete with five ventilation shafts was built. It was the site of the worst construction accident on the line, when a section collapsed on 2nd July 1861, killing five men.

The route met some very challenging terrain along the Wye Valley between Hassop and Buxton that required two viaducts and eight tunnels. The first of these, the 533-yard Headstone tunnel, emerges into a very short cutting then straight onto the Headstone viaduct, one of the most dramatic and well-known features of the line, that crosses the Wye Valley at a point where the valley curves round almost ninety degrees at Monsal Head. The spoil from the tunnel was used to build foundations for the easternmost pillar of the viaduct, which needed extensive repairs in 1907 after slippage.

The viaduct came in for heavy criticism at the time of construction, including that of the poet and conservationist John Ruskin, who condemned the building of the railway in his *Fors Clavigera: Letters to the Workmen and Labourers of Great Britain*:

'There was a rocky valley between Buxton and Bakewell, once upon a time, divine as the Vale of Tempe… You Enterprised a Railroad through the valley – you blasted its rocks away, heaped thousands of tons of shale into its lovely stream. The valley is gone, and the Gods with it; and now, every fool in Buxton can be in Bakewell in half an hour, and every fool in Bakewell at Buxton; which you think a lucrative process of exchange – you Fools everywhere.'

When the railway closed and the demolition of the viaduct was proposed, there was considerable opposition. In 1970 it was protected with a Grade II listing.

The route continues through two more tunnels, Cressbrook and Litton, at 471 and 515 yards respectively. They cut off some of the meanderings of the River Wye as the line continues to its summit, just east of Millers Dale.

The route then descends slightly, crossing twin viaducts into Millers Dale station. This somewhat isolated location, 800 feet above sea level, developed into a busy station. From 1867 many of the MR's express services stopped there, it being the interchange for services to Buxton. It was decided that, with Buxton being a terminus, the additional time required to reverse services out of the station was unnecessary and instead a shuttle service to Millers Dale was provided to link with the express services from London to Manchester in addition to the branch line service. Some expresses from London also had a Buxton coach attached at the rear, which was uncoupled at Millers Dale and attached to the shuttle service.

New platform shelters, run round loops and a subway linking the platforms were added throughout the 1870s and 1880s. Between 1902 and 1905 there was a major development when extra running lines were added.

When originally constructed, the line had just one viaduct, with two running lines. The development saw a new viaduct being added, on the northern side of the existing one. This provided two extra running lines, allowing trains to be routed onto fast or slow routes, enabling express and freight trains to overtake stopping services. The station was also extended at this point, giving it a total of five platforms, one for each line and a bay for the branch line services to Buxton. Once the construction of the additional viaduct was complete, the original one was closed for strengthening and maintenance, finally reopening in 1906 with all four lines operational.

Further westwards the line met more engineering challenges, where a limestone spur blocked progress. As the narrow, steep-sided gorge was not large enough to accommodate the trackbed, two tunnels were constructed, Chee Tor Number One and Two tunnels, with a viaduct between them. After this point a narrow ledge carved out of the valley side gave just enough room for the twin tracks to be laid before encountering another tunnel, the 94-yard-long Rusher Cutting Tunnel.

At the point where the Buxton branch turned southwest, the main line continued northwest, and a triangular junction was created, with three signal boxes controlling traffic. This was also the site of Blackwell Mill Halt, one of the smallest stations in Britain, built to service the row of railway worker's cottages that had been constructed inside the triangle and which are still inhabited today.

Heading into Buxton, two more tunnels were needed: Pic Tor, 191 yards long, and Ashwood, 100 yards long. Finally, the long, curved Ashwood Dale Viaduct led under the LNWR line into Buxton station, with a spur later added that headed north to join the LNWR line. The original Midland station site at Buxton had a goods shed, engine shed and various facilities. The engine shed was closed in 1935 and amalgamated with the former LNWR shed, as both companies had become part of the London, Midland & Scottish Railway at the grouping of Britain's railway companies in 1923.

The line reached Hassop in 1862 and Buxton in 1863. At the same time, the LNWR opened its own station in Buxton, adjacent to the Midland one. Watching the developments of both railway companies approaching their town, Buxton's councillors were concerned that the two stations could spoil the town's character and engaged architect Joseph Paxton to come up with an acceptable solution. Paxton, most famous for designing the Crystal Palace, was already well known in the area, as he had previously been head gardener at Chatsworth House and designed the Grand Pavilion there in 1840. His solution to the station design was a pair of adjacent and almost identical train sheds built from local stone with a wrought iron glazed roof and fronted with identical half-circle fanlight windows, the name of each railway company being carved in the stonework surrounding each window.

Both stations formally opened on 1st June 1863, with Paxton famously attending grand lunches at both ceremonies. *The Advertiser* of Saturday 6th June, 1863 commented: 'Buxton enters upon a new era in its history. From being a remote spot, hidden among the hills of the Peak, to be approached only by a serious expenditure of time and money, it is now but five hours from London, and will soon be only one from Manchester!'

Paxton also designed the original Rowsley station building in 1849, however, this was replaced in 1862, as the new alignment of the line didn't fit the alignment of the old station, which would have been fine if the route had continued via Chatsworth as originally planned. The new building was built in a much grander style than the previous one, as the station was preferred by visitors to Chatsworth House. The name was changed to 'Rowsley for Chatsworth' in 1867, which continued until 1965.

The new station had two platforms, later linked by a subway in 1891. It has been speculated that the subway was built to protect visiting dignitaries from inclement weather. It saw a large number of titled visitors, including royalty, with King Edward VII and Queen Alexandra being regular visitors to Chatsworth.

The old station building became a goods station, known as 'The Old Yard', and continued in use until 1968. As a Grade II listed building, it survived, whilst all other buildings in the yard were demolished. It was used for a while by a business renting The Old Yard and was restored to become part of the Peak Shopping Centre, which opened in 1999.

The other station on the line used by landed gentry was Bakewell, the closest station to Haddon Hall, home of the Duke of Rutland. The Rutland coat of arms was carved into the stone facade of the station. Initially the Duke was against the railway, as were many of the landed gentry, but due to lobbying by the citizens of Bakewell, he relented and allowed the station to be built. The station featured identical ornate iron and glass platform canopies to Rowsley, both far grander than one would expect for a small rural station, owing to the patronage of local estate owners. Bakewell had an annual influx of visitors for the Bakewell Show, a large agriculture, horticulture and forestry show, which saw special trains laid on to Bakewell from numerous locations.

Another station built in a grander style than usual was Great Longstone, which was designed by William Barlow, consultant engineer for the MR and designer of St Pancras station. The ornate station building was designed to complement the adjacent Thornbridge Hall, which was owned by George Marples, one of the MR directors. The station incorporated a private set of steps from the hall to allow him direct access to the Down platform. It saw little traffic and closed earlier than the rest of the line, in 1962. However, a local nurse relied on the station and was given a key to allow her access for the 8.05 train. Upon closure the station was sold and became a private residence.

The largest yard on the line was that at Rowsley. When the line first opened there were sidings for locomotives and a small depot. It was soon apparent that larger facilities were needed, with plans drawn up in 1874 for an extensive area of sidings. These were brought into use several months before the official opening in 1877. This was followed by an extension to the loco depot in 1878 from one road to four, with the addition of a coaling stage. During the 1880s and 1890s the MR also constructed around 50 cottages in Rowsley for its workers. One of the attractions of working on the railway was the opportunity of a job for life as well as reasonable housing provision, the standard of most railway company houses being higher than that of private landlords.

Despite the development and enlargement of the Rowsley site, it was apparent that a much larger depot was needed. Although estimates were received for the work in 1914, the outbreak of World War I delayed the project, with the MR finally signing contracts in 1922. The new depot was completed by 1924, apart from the coaling plant, completion of which delayed the depot becoming fully operational until July 1926.

One of the purposes of Rowsley shed was to provide engines for banking of heavy goods trains. Freight was an important part of the MR's traffic, with coal trains heading to the industrial areas of the North West from the East Midlands coalfield. The line out of Rowsley climbs almost 600 feet before it reaches Buxton, mostly at a gradient of 1 in 100. These severe gradients required the additional locomotives, known as bankers, to push freight trains up this section.

The line was also the route of several fast express trains, including named trains such as the *Peak Express*, *Palatine* and the *Midland Pullman*. These were hauled by some of the LMSR's finest locomotives, such as the Jubilee and Patriot classes, along with the occasional Royal Scot.

In 1954 British Rail produced a report entitled *Modernisation and Re-Equipment of the British Railways*, which advocated wholesale scrapping of steam traction, replacing it with diesel haulage, except on main routes, which would be electrified. The Peak Line was one of those briefly considered for electrification, but the plan went no further. Another report proposed changing the line to diesel haulage, although the depot at Rowsley was only ever allocated two Sulzer Type 2 locos to assist with banking duties. They arrived in 1965, after the shed had lost most of its loco allocation to Derby.

The line did see other diesel traction, however, when it was used by the *Midland Pullman*. Launched in July 1960, this was a luxury all-first-class train that used six-car diesel electric units to operate a fast Manchester-London business travel service during the period when the West Coast Main Line was disrupted during electrification. It only stopped at Cheadle Heath (now closed) and managed the journey from London to Manchester in a record 3 hours 15 minutes. Its speed impacted other services on the Peak line, as it needed two block signalling sections clear ahead of it instead of the usual one section other trains required. It was withdrawn in 1966, being replaced by the *Manchester Pullman* on the newly electrified West Coast Main Line, cutting the London to Manchester journey time even further, down to 2 hours 30 minutes.

In 1962 the government published *The Reshaping of Britain's Railways*, more commonly called the Beeching Report. The recommendations included the closure of two-thirds of Britain's unprofitable lines, leaving the remaining system to pay its way. It listed the stopping services between Ambergate and Chinley as ones that would be withdrawn, with through services between Ambergate and Stockport continuing, however, the protests of the local inhabitants managed to defer these closures. There were still some through trains from Buxton to London St Pancras, though the majority only went as far as Millers Dale.

Closure was to come a few years later, starting with Rowsley sidings and goods depot in 1964. The intermediate stations at Millers Dale, Bakewell, Rowsley and Darley Dale followed, closing in March 1967, along with services to Buxton, despite pleas from ramblers to keep them open. Complete closure was sanctioned by

Barbara Castle, the then Minister for Transport, between Peak Forest and Matlock, which took place on 14th July 1968. The remaining through passenger services were diverted via Chesterfield and the Hope Valley line. The track removal began in 1969 and the Midland station at Buxton was demolished to allow the construction of a relief road.

The Buxton end of the line still carries freight traffic on the section from Buxton viaduct through Blackwell Mill junction, where the former LNWR side of the junction is still used, the other two having been removed on closure. Known as the Great Rocks freight line, it passes through the extensive quarry workings at Tunstead Cement Plant and Dove Holes quarry before joining the main line at Chinley South Junction. Buxton's former LNWR station is still open, with hourly services to Manchester via Stockport. At the other end of the disused section, trains from Derby and Nottingham terminate at Matlock. In 1975, rail enthusiasts formed the Peak Railway Society with the intention of restoring the line as a heritage railway. After several years of negotiations and fundraising, in 1981 the derelict Buxton Midland site was purchased and turned into a Steam Centre. A decade later, with the southern portion of the line between Darley Dale and Matlock (Riverside) open for public services, Buxton Steam Centre was closed, and parts of the land sold, which allowed line restoration to continue from Darley Dale. Rowsley was reached in 1997 and now the railway has redeveloped the former Rowsley engine shed site as its main base and northern terminus.

Much of the remainder of the line was taken over by the Peak District National Park Authority in 1980 and turned into the very popular Monsal Trail, a walking and cycling route. It covers about 8½ miles of the former railway, between the Topley Pike junction in Wye Dale, three miles east of Buxton, and runs to Coombs Viaduct, one mile south-east of Bakewell.

For many years the trail was diverted away from the tunnels at Monsal Head and Cressbrook, which had been closed for safety reasons. Finally, in May 2011, the tunnels were reopened after considerable conservation works.

The reopening of the line has been discussed for over two decades or more. There was a feasibility study in 2004, which, along with many other rail reopening studies, failed to take the wider economic and social benefits of the reopening into account, but did say that the route offered 'the only, practical, segregated route through the area for public transport. Its condition overall is very good and reinstatement of a railway would not incur the need for the significant "new construction" activity that would be required on any other alignment.'

Since then there have been two bids for funding as part of the 'Reopening Our Railways' funds, but these have been unsuccessful.

In a slight irony regarding the original and current uses of the line, 14,000 people signed a petition in 2021 against its reopening due to the existence of the Monsal Trail and its tourism and recreational benefits, however, 19,000 did support a petition in favour of reopening.

MATLOCK

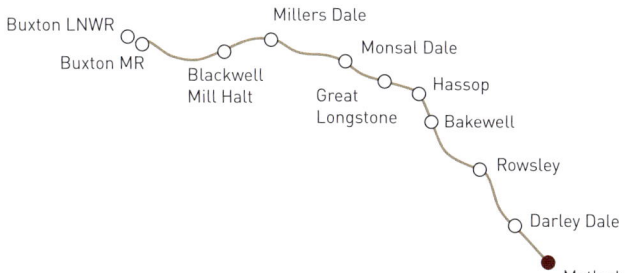

Stanier Black 5 No 44753 arrives at Matlock in 1949, with what appears to be a party of walkers on the platform and a gentleman wearing a black armband. The unusual appearance of the loco, with the large steam pipes at the front of the smokebox, shows it is one of 20 experimental Black Fives built with Caprotti valve gear by British Railways between 1948 and 1951. The design differed from the usual Walschearts valve gear by driving a gearbox with a single shaft, located between the frames, that was operated by a bevel gear on the leading coupled axle. This drove a camshaft and poppet valves and was more efficient at high speeds, though the locos tended to have slower acceleration. Only two locomotives with Caprotti gear survived into preservation, British Railway Standard Class 5MT 4-6-0 locomotive No 73129 and BR Standard 8P No 7100 *Duke of Gloucester*.

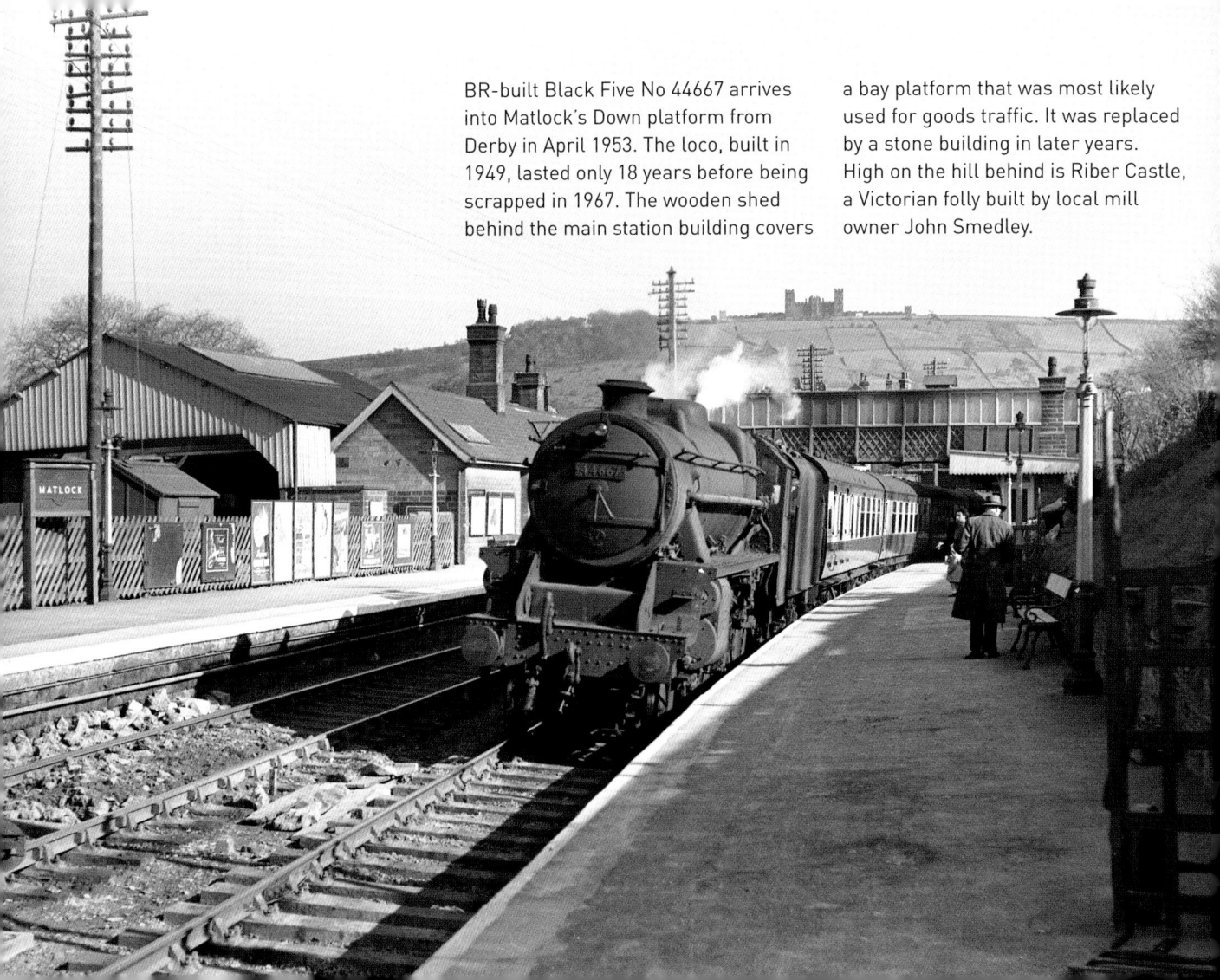

BR-built Black Five No 44667 arrives into Matlock's Down platform from Derby in April 1953. The loco, built in 1949, lasted only 18 years before being scrapped in 1967. The wooden shed behind the main station building covers a bay platform that was most likely used for goods traffic. It was replaced by a stone building in later years. High on the hill behind is Riber Castle, a Victorian folly built by local mill owner John Smedley.

Ex-LMS Jubilee Class 4-6-0 No 45611 *Hong Kong* arrives at Matlock with the 2.30pm Liverpool Central to Nottingham train on 25th July 1959. This class of locomotive, of which 190 were built, was designed by William Stanier for express passenger work. The coach in the background appears to be an ex-MR clerestory compartment coach, dating from the early part of the 20th century. The gentlemen on the platform awaiting the train's arrival are travelling with what appears to be fishing rods and tackle boxes.

DARLEY DALE

A view from the road level of Darley Dale signal box and crossing gates. This is a Type 2 MR signal box, of timber construction. The MR was always fiercely independent and signalling was no exception. They were one of only four pre-grouping railway companies to set up their own signal works, at Derby. By 1870 the company was producing their own signal boxes instead of relying on either specialist signalling contractors or local builders, as was the case with many other railways.

Midland signal boxes were standardised and prefabricated at Derby and transported to site on a special train. New signal boxes could be very quickly erected and in a special exercise in 1920 they carried out the task in a mere 85 minutes! The basic designs changed very little and were perpetuated by the LMS after the 1923 grouping of the railway companies.

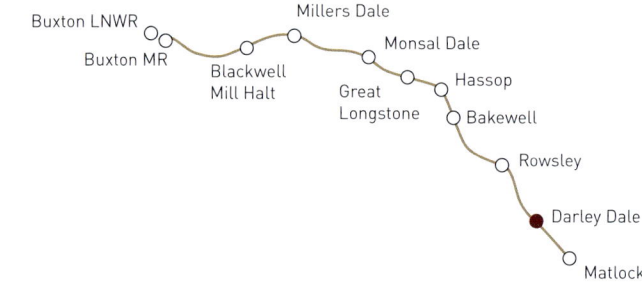

Darley Dale Station, viewed from the Up platform. Built in Gothic Revival style in local stone, it was officially known as Darley until October 1890. The first station building was south of what is now Station Road, and the main building, almost certainly designed by Paxton, is still standing, but is a private residence. In 1874 the current station was built, north of the level crossing. The contract for erection of the station was awarded to Joseph Glossop and the final cost was £2,247.17s. The footbridge was added later, in 1910, but was removed when the line closed. The station continues to be used as an intermediate stop on the Peak Rail heritage railway. The loco arriving is No 41143, an ex-MR Compound 4-4-0 on a Derby to Manchester service in July 1957.

An ex-MR Fowler 4F No 44129 passes through the level crossing at Darley Dale in June 1958. The first wagon is carrying a new David Brown Albion baler, presumably a delivery for a farm on the line. The original station was situated on this side of the crossing. The signals on the right are original MR examples, installed before the creation of the LMS in 1923. The coach that can be seen beyond the signal box is a converted railway carriage known as a camping coach. It was on this site between 1934 and the early 1960s and could be rented for holidays. There were over 200 camping coaches across the railway network between the 1930s and 1960s, including two others on this line, at Bakewell and Hassop. The extensive goods sidings served several stone quarrying companies in the town, including private sidings into company premises. The station was renamed Darley Dale from the earlier Darley in 1880, however, the company timetables didn't feature the new name until 1890.

ROWSLEY

Two ex-MR 3F 0-6-0s and an LMS Stanier 8F sit outside Rowsley shed in February 1949. It was well equipped when built in the early 1920s, with locker rooms and hot baths, which most of the nearby railway cottages did not have at the time. The original capacity of 24 locomotives in the shed was exceeded within a decade. By the end of World War II there were 60 locomotives crammed into the shed and surrounding sidings, and with over 220 footplate staff the original 140 lockers proved inadequate. The yard was still being improved in the early 1950s, with an extra run round line to the turntable added in 1955 and the shed roof being renewed in 1959. Less than a decade later, in 1968, the demolition team had completed their work and the entire facility was a pile of rubble.

Rowsley motive power depot, date unknown, showing the turntable and coaling stage. The locomotive resting on the turntable is an ex-MR 0-6-0 Johnson class 3F, built in 1885. This class numbered over 900 locomotives, with many surviving into the British Railways era. The coaling stage in the background was built in 1924-5 and could coal two locomotives at once. Coal wagons were tipped into smaller hoppers alongside, which were then hauled up the rails that can be seen on the right-hand side of the structure, before being tipped over into the main holding silo before being released into the locomotive below. The construction of this plant was somewhat delayed, one of several factors holding back the opening of the MR's flagship depot by 18 months, showing that delays to large infrastructure projects are nothing new!

Rowsley shed, seen here in April 1958, was the main motive power depot on the line and accommodated banking engines to assist freight trains on the severe gradients. There was a large marshalling yard adjacent to the shed for holding and assembling freight trains. A variety of motive power can be seen, including a 4MT 2-6-4 Tank, an LMS 3F tank, an ex-North London 2F tank (used on the Cromford & High Peak Line), a 2-6-0 'Crab' and what are probably Class 3F and 4F 0-6-0s with their tenders facing the photographer. The two snowploughs mounted on their stands and the pile of braziers by the buffer stop indicate that the photo was not taken in the winter. Braziers were often used to keep water cranes from freezing in the cold weather.

The structure on the platform was the original Rowsley station, designed by Joseph Paxton for the opening of the MBM&MJ in May 1849. It operated as a passenger station for just a few years, until 1862, as the new alignment of the railway took it on a different route as it continued to Buxton. It then became the goods depot and was later known as The Old Yard when the new goods sidings and marshalling yard opened near the new station in 1877. It still handled a large amount of traffic, mainly timber, stone and agricultural produce and an increasing amount of milk when Express Dairies opened a processing plant next door to the yard in 1933. It continued in use for goods traffic until 1968, when the redundant yard was leased by a transport company and it became their offices. It was awarded Grade II listed building status in 1972. In the 1990s the whole site was developed as the Peak Village shopping centre, of which the building became a feature.

Rowsley Station, looking at the Up platform in 1953. Opened in 1862 to replace the original building, it featured much more lavish facilities than one would expect for a rural station of this size, as it was used by a large number of dignitaries visiting the Duke of Devonshire's nearby home, Chatsworth House. The name was changed to Rowsley for Chatsworth in 1867, which lasted until 1965. The two platforms were linked by a subway in 1891. It is speculated that the subway was built to protect visiting dignitaries from inclement weather. The station saw a large number of titled visitors, including royalty, with King Edward VII and Queen Alexandra being regular visitors to Chatsworth. The station canopies are of the same design as those at Bakewell, also a station designed for visiting dignitaries to the Duke of Rutland's home at Haddon Hall.

An ex-London & North Western Railway Class G2a, No 49281, with a Down mixed goods train near Rowsley, recorded in September 1961. This is a good example of a mixed freight, with predominantly mineral wagons and the addition of a tank and some covered goods wagons towards the rear of the train, along with a larger hopper wagon. This loco, built in 1918, one of 320 of this class inherited by BR, survived until December 1962.

BAKEWELL

An ex-War Department Austerity class 2-8-0 heads through Bakewell station with a train of empty mineral wagons. These heavy freight 2-8-0 locomotives were designed by Robert Riddles and built in large numbers from 1943 onwards. Riddles was a deputy to William Stanier, Chief Mechanical Engineer of the LMS, but moved to the War Office in 1939, where he became Director of Transportation Equipment and designed the Austerity locomotives. This view of Bakewell shows the outline of the former canopy on the stonework of the platform facade.

An ex-MR 0-6-0 built by Beyer Peacock in 1884, No 58228 is seen passing through Bakewell in June 1958.
The canopy of the Up platform has already been removed, along with the two outermost sections of the Down platform canopy. The station building featured the coat of arms of the Duke of Rutland, who lived at nearby Haddon Hall and used the station on a regular basis. The station is already showing signs of neglect and disrepair, with several of the ornate ridge tiles on the roof missing.

HASSOP

A view of Hassop station on an unknown date looking north from the Up platform. Station staff and a permanent way maintenance man pose for the camera. Although the station was built primarily for the benefit of the Duke of Devonshire at Chatsworth House some 3½ miles away, it saw little use, as the Duke and his visitors preferred to use Rowsley, despite the station bearing the name Hassop for Chatsworth for some of its working life. It hosted an LMS camping coach in the 1930s and finally closed in 1942, although the goods yard continued to operate until 1964. The building survived and today forms part of a complex containing a cafe, bookshop and cycle hire centre for visitors to the Monsal Trail. The small weighbridge building and station master's house have also survived.

GREAT LONGSTONE

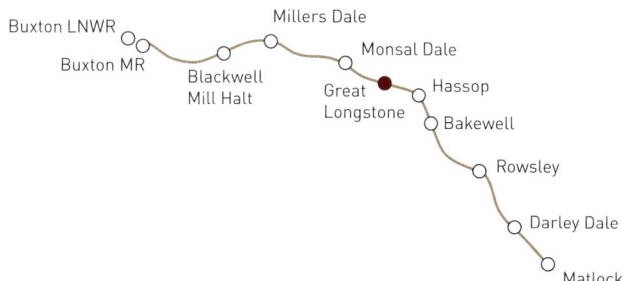

Great Longstone station is particularly distinctive, with its rich architectural decoration. Designed by William Barlow, consultant engineer for the MR, it opened in 1863. The adjacent Thornbridge Hall was owned by George Marples, one of the MR directors, and the station incorporated a private set of steps from the hall to allow him direct access to the Down platform. The station saw little traffic and closed earlier than the rest of the line, in 1962. However, a local nurse relied on the station and was given a key to allow her access for the 8.05 train. All services were withdrawn in 1967 and the station was sold to become a private residence.

Ex-LMS Crab 2-6-0 No 42887 exits Headstone Tunnel in September 1950. The 533-yard-long tunnel has a cutting with near vertical sides on its eastern approach, which today has been given the designation of a Site of Special Scientific Interest thanks to its distinctive rock strata. The western portal opens out into a much shorter cutting for around 50 yards before the line reaches the Headstone viaduct. It was reopened in 2011 to walkers and cyclists as part of the Monsal Trail.

Right: A southbound express passes over Headstone viaduct hauled by a Sulzer Type 4 diesel, D18. It was later renumbered 45121 and withdrawn from service in November 1987, being scrapped at Crewe works in 1993.

An unidentified BR Standard 9F 2-10-0 on Headstone viaduct over the River Wye in Monsal Dale is seen at the head of a southbound mineral train on Wednesday 15th August 1962. Each of the five arches spans 50 feet (15.5m) and is roughly 25m tall. The viaduct was designed by William Barlow, consultant engineer for the MR's southern extension from Bedford to London, including the layout of their London terminus station at St Pancras, for which he also designed the station roof, a 240ft-wide self-supporting cast iron structure.

MONSAL DALE

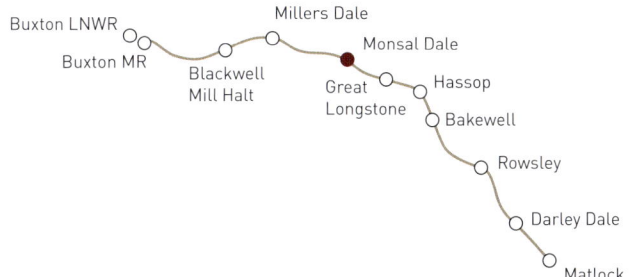

An ex-LMS 2-6-0 Hughes-designed 2-6-0, No 42792, arrives at Monsal Dale station, September 1957. When the line opened, a siding was provided at Cressbrook, at the request of a local mill owner. A station was later built there and the name changed to Monsal Dale. It was built into the hillside, with the Down line and platform seen in the photo built on a shelf carved into the rock face, but the wooden Up platform the photographer is standing on was built on trestles over the hillside.
Out of shot is a simple wooden station building that was moved from Evesham in Worcestershire in 1866. It was never a very busy station, the majority of passengers using it being ramblers accessing the Peak District. It closed to regular passenger traffic in 1959, but saw occasional ramblers' specials and excursions until April 1961.

MILLERS DALE

The second viaduct at Millers Dale is under construction here in September 1904. The masonry piers are mostly complete and the first pair of girders is being assembled on temporary staging. The crane on the staging is actually a hand-powered rail crane on temporary rails. To the right, the timber formwork for a masonry arch is being constructed. There is another temporary track and shed in the foreground and a steam crane on another set of temporary rails running between the pillars behind the shed. Note the lifting derrick in the foreground, the rear legs held in place by large piles of masonry.

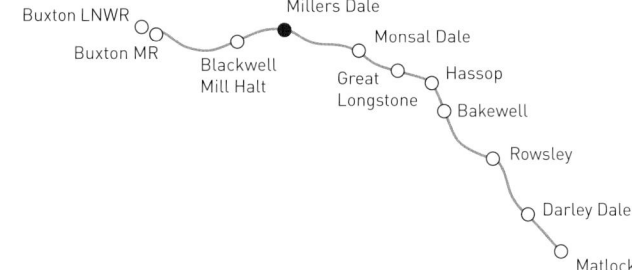

A view of Millers Dale station looking West towards Buxton in 1912. The viaduct nearest the photographer was the first one built, opening in 1863. The furthest one was added in 1902-1905 to expand the line's capacity. The addition of the second viaduct at Millers Dale meant that now fast and slow lines in both directions ran through the station, enabling fast trains to proceed rather than waiting behind stopping services. The original viaduct was closed for a year after the new one had opened, allowing it to be refurbished and strengthened. It then carried the Down fast (the outer line) and Down slow lines, with the new viaduct carrying the Up lines. The station master's house stands on the small hill behind the station, giving a good view of the entire station and its activity. Both viaducts survive to this day, with the original one being part of the Monsal Trail walking and cycling route. The newer structure is fenced off.

The *Midland Pullman* passes through Millers Dale in July 1961. Launched in July 1960, this was a luxury all-first-class service that used two new Blue Pullman six-car diesel-electric units to operate a fast Manchester-London business travel service while services on the West Coast Main Line were disrupted because of its electrification. It called only at Cheadle Heath and made the journey from London to Manchester in a record 3 hours 15 minutes. The service was withdrawn in 1966, replaced by the electric loco-hauled *Manchester Pullman* from Manchester Piccadilly to Euston on the newly electrified West Coast Main Line, cutting the journey time even further, to 2 hours 30 minutes.

Matlock to Buxton 49

A Park Royal railbus at Millers Dale. In the late 1950s, British Railways tested a series of small railbuses produced by a variety of manufacturers as cheaper alternatives to using conventional locomotives on lines that had low levels of use. Park Royal, better known for building bus bodies, built five of this model, which were initially allocated to the London Midland Region. These 42ft-long vehicles were powered by a 150hp AEC engine with manual transmission. As with many other railbuses, they eventually ended up on the Scottish Region, but were withdrawn in the late 1960s and scrapped. The station was renamed Millers Dale for Tideswell in 1889 (the village of Tideswell is two miles north of the station and a much larger settlement than Millers Dale). Most of the activity at Millers Dale was as an interchange for passengers heading to and from Buxton.

An ex-LMS Stanier 8F freight loco, No 48225, hauls a mineral train through Millers Dale station in August 1960. This locomotive was one of many LMS engines built by other works during World War II, in this case by the North British Locomotive Company of Glasgow. The extent of the station buildings at Millers Dale can be seen clearly here, with platforms for expresses from London and Manchester to stop, allowing passengers to change for Buxton. The Buxton services ran from platform 5, which is the furthest right in the photo. The goods yard and goods shed can be seen on the left. The station building survives as a cafe and visitor centre, despite half of it being a shell, and the goods shed has been restored.

The spectacular landscape through which the line passed is captured in this view taken from a vantage point above the first of the Chee Tor tunnels. Looking east back towards Millers Dale station, a mixed goods train headed by an LMS Class 4F 0-6-0 is passing an unidentified Peak class diesel in charge of a Manchester-bound express on Friday 2nd August 1963.

52 Lost Lines of England

BLACKWELL MILL HALT

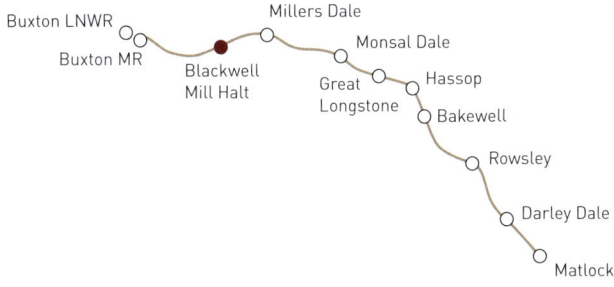

An unidentified Stanier 8F 2-8-0 passes Blackwell Mill Halt with a brakevan on Friday 2nd August 1963. This was one of the smallest stations in the country and was built to serve the small row of railway cottages which nestled in the triangular junction. It was served by the shuttle trains which ran between Millers Dale and Buxton, the two other sides of the junction having no station. The 8F is under the control of an MR lower quadrant signal. The one on the right protected the curve from Peak Forest Junction to Buxton Junction, now the only track remaining at this site. The station closed in 1966.

An unidentified BR Standard 5MT 4-6-0 battles up the gradient at Millers Dale Junction with a Down goods train on Friday 2nd August 1963. It has just left Chee Dale and passed Millers Dale Junction signalbox, which can just be seen to the right of the end of the train, and is taking the main line to Peak Forest and Manchester. The line to the right was to Buxton, while Blackwell Mill Halt was behind the camera position.

Members of the photographer's family take up most of the available space at Blackwell Mill Halt on Friday 2nd August 1963. As this halt served the railway staff cottages it did not appear in any public timetables, although it was included in working timetables from 1874 and operated as a request stop. The section of track through the halt was lifted in 1968, with the adjacent side of the triangle remaining in operational use as a freight line to this day. The platforms are extant, but overgrown, and the railway cottages have been refurbished and are in private ownership.

BUXTON

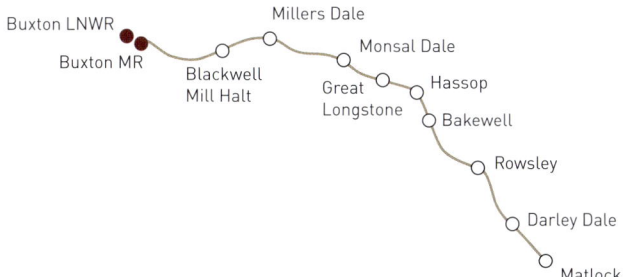

This photograph shows the matching London North Western Railway and MR stations at Buxton, the MR station being the furthest from the camera. Each had the railway company's name carved in the stone surround of the fanlight window. Although in the earlier years there was an intense rivalry between the two companies, as the railway network matured they realised that cooperation would be beneficial to both and in 1908 signed a traffic agreement to enable joint working and the elimination of wasteful practice. The result for Buxton was the two stations being managed as one, under the control of MR station master Mr Samuel Pitt. The wall of the LNWR station with the fanlight window survives, however, the canopy was demolished in the late 1960s along with the entire Midland station, the site of which has now been obliterated by a relief road.

This view shows the Buxton shed originally opened by the LNWR, close to the MR one. Although both companies operated their sheds independently even after the 1908 traffic agreement, when the railways were grouped into the 'Big Four' in 1923, moves were made to minimise duplication of resources and by 1935 the overcrowded former Midland shed was closed and loco operations were transferred to the former LNWR shed, which had been extended for the purpose. The lines surrounding the shed contain various facilities, including ash pits, coaling and watering facilities and a turntable, with a mixture of former LNWR and MR locomotives.

A class 100 Diesel Multiple Unit at Buxton in 1961. These DMUs, built by Gloucester Carriage and Wagon Co, operated on Manchester-Buxton-Crewe routes as well as local services on the Peak Forest Line. The station porter appears to be unloading mailbags into an electric platform trolley. Note the decorative castings along the top of the walls and the cast iron columns supporting the roof. Paxton's design for this station shows similarities to his former LNWR station at Oxford, which was controversially dismantled and moved in 1998.

A group of boys watch a loco crew prepare No 41905, a William Stanier-designed 0-4-4 tank loco. It appears the loco has just been coaled up, judging by the almost overflowing coal bunker. Buxton Midland station had an unusual design feature where the centre platform under the original train shed had two platforms facing onto it. In the background is the extension to the train shed, which was built in 1886. The adjacent station operated by the LNWR became jointly managed with the Midland one in 1908, after the two companies came to an agreement to cooperate in various areas to cut their costs and prevent duplication of services. It wasn't until 1923, when both companies were absorbed into the newly founded London Midland & Scottish Railway, that the two Buxton stations were wholly operated as one station, with the platforms being renumbered across both, starting with platform 1 at the far side of the former LNWR building and ending with platform 6 in the background of this photo.

Matlock to Buxton 63

CREDITS

Lost Lines of England – Matlock to Buxton

Published in Great Britain in 2025 by Graffeg Limited.

ISBN 9781802583472

Text by G. P. Essex copyright © 2025. Designed and produced by Graffeg Limited copyright © 2025.

Graffeg Limited, 15 Neptune Court, Vanguard Way, Cardiff, CF24 5PJ, Wales, UK. Tel: 01554 824000. croeso@graffeg.com. www.graffeg.com.

G. P. Essex is hereby identified as the author of this work in accordance with section 77 of the Copyright, Designs and Patents Act 1988.

Printed by 1010 Printing, China.

A CIP Catalogue record for this book is available from the British Library.

All rights reserved. No part of this publication may be reproduced, stored in a retrieval system or transmitted, in any form or by any means, electronic, mechanical, photocopying, recording or otherwise, without the prior permission of the publishers.

This book is designed for general readers, printed with materials and processes that are safe and meet all applicable European safety requirements. The book does not contain elements that could pose health or safety risks under normal and intended use.

We hereby declare that this product complies with all applicable requirements of the General Product Safety Regulation (GPSR) and any other relevant EU legislation.

Appointed EU Representative:
Easy Access System Europe Oü, 16879218
Mustamäe tee 50, 10621, Tallinn, Estonia
gpsr.requests@easproject.com

1 2 3 4 5 6 7 8 9

Photo credits

© Online Transport Archive: pages 14, 16, 28, 31, 38.

© Transport Treasury: pages 17, 20, 23, 24, 42, 48, 50, 62.

© Kidderminster Railway Museum: pages 19, 25, 35, 36, 39, 45, 58, 61.

© Colour Rail: pages 21, 32, 63.

© John Alsop Collection: pages 26, 27, 47.

© Geoff Plumb: pages 41, 53, 54, 56, 57.

© Colin Boocock: page 51.

The photographs used in this book have come from a variety of sources. Wherever possible contributors have been identified although some images may have been used without credit or acknowledgement and if this is the case apologies are offered and full credit will be given in any future edition.

Cover: Bakewell.
Back cover: Rowsley, Millers Dale, Buxton.

G. P. Essex is a writer and photographer specialising in railways. His website can be found at www.randomrailways.com.

Lost Tramways UK and Ireland series:
www.graffeg.com

Lost Lines of England:
Birmingham to Oxford ISBN 9781912654871
Birmingham to Worcester ISBN 9781802583489
Matlock to Buxton ISBN ISBN 9781802583472
Ryde to Cowes ISBN 9781912654864
Stratford-upon-Avon to Gloucester ISBN 9781802582024
The Cheddar Valley Line ISBN 9781913134402

Lost Lines of England and Wales:
Shrewsbury to Chester ISBN 9781914079122
Wye Valley ISBN 9781802582017

Lost Lines of Wales series:
Aberystwyth to Carmarthen ISBN 9781909823198
Bangor to Afon Wen ISBN 9781922213115
Brecon to Newport ISBN 9781909823181
Cambrian Coast Line ISBN 9781909823204
Chester to Holyhead ISBN 9781912050697
Conwy Valley Line ISBN 9781912654147
Llandovery to Craven Arms ISBN 9781914079115
Monmouthshire Eastern Valley ISBN 9781802581089
Monmouthshire Western Valley ISBN 9781802581102
Rhyl to Corwen ISBN 9781912213108
Ruabon to Barmouth ISBN 9781909823174
Shrewsbury to Aberystwyth ISBN 9781912050680
Swansea to Llandovery ISBN 9781914079108
The Heads of the Valleys Line ISBN 9781912654154
The Mid Wales Line ISBN 9781912050673
Vale of Neath ISBN 9781912050666

Scan the QR code to see the Lost Lines collection. Also eBooks available for Kindle and Apple Books.